The Ultimate Guide to Earning Money & Financial Freedom

Arvie Del mundo

Published by Arvie Del mundo, 2025.

THE ULTIMATE GUIDE TO EARNING MONEY & FINANCIAL FREEDOM

First edition. February 18, 2025.

ISBN: 979-8230841685

Written by Arvie Del mundo.

Also by Arvie Del mundo

The Creation of Infiverse with Bible Verses
The Existence of God - A Comprehensive Guide
The Existence of God: A Comprehensive Guide 2nd Edition
The Ultimate Guide to Earning Money & Financial Freedom

Book Title: The Ultimate Guide to Earning Money & Financial Freedom

Author: Arvie Del Mundo

Dedication

This book is dedicated to all the dreamers, hustlers, and visionaries who refuse to settle for less. To those who believe in their potential and are willing to take the necessary steps toward financial independence, this book is for you.

To my family and friends, whose unwavering support and encouragement have been a source of strength, I am deeply grateful. Your belief in me has been the driving force behind this work.

To the aspiring entrepreneurs, freelancers, and investors who strive for success despite challenges, may this book serve as a guiding light on your journey to financial freedom.

Finally, to the relentless seekers of knowledge and those who dare to challenge the norm, remember—wealth is not just about money; it's about the choices, freedom, and impact you create.

Let this book be a stepping stone to a prosperous and fulfilling future.

INTRODUCTION: THE PATH to Financial Success

Why This Book?

Earning money is not just about hard work—it's about working smart. In today's fast-changing world, financial success requires a combination of skills, knowledge, and strategic planning. Whether you're an aspiring entrepreneur, a freelancer, an investor, or simply someone looking to improve your financial situation, this book will serve as your step-by-step guide to achieving wealth and stability.

WHAT YOU WILL LEARN

Proven business strategies to maximize profits.

The secrets of investing wisely in stocks, real estate, and digital assets.

How to build multiple income streams for financial security.

Practical ways to leverage digital marketing to boost earnings.

Essential tips for sales, negotiation, and personal branding.

WHO IS THIS BOOK FOR?

Entrepreneurs looking to scale their businesses.

Freelancers and remote workers aiming for financial independence.

Investors seeking smart wealth-building techniques.

Anyone who wants to break free from financial struggles and create a stable income.

HOW TO USE THIS BOOK

Each chapter is designed to provide practical, actionable steps that you can apply immediately. The book is structured to cater to different earning methods, ensuring you find strategies that best fit your goals. Whether you are a beginner or an experienced professional, this book will help you level up your financial journey.

Chapter 1: Mindset of Financial Success

The Foundation of Wealth Begins in the Mind

Success in earning money is not just about strategies, investments, or skills—it starts with the right mindset. Many of the world's wealthiest individuals developed a mindset that allowed them to recognize opportunities, overcome challenges, and build lasting wealth. In this chapter, we will explore how to cultivate a financial success mindset that will set the foundation for your journey to financial freedom.

1. THE DIFFERENCE BETWEEN the Wealthy and the Poor Mindset

Wealthy people and those who struggle financially often have vastly different ways of thinking about money. Let's examine key differences:

Scarcity vs. Abundance Mentality – Those with a scarcity mindset believe there is never enough money, while those with an abundance mindset see money as limitless and opportunities everywhere.

Risk Aversion vs. Calculated Risk-Taking – Fear of failure stops many from taking action, while the wealthy understand that calculated risks lead to success.

Spending vs. Investing – Poor financial habits lead people to spend money as soon as they get it, while the wealthy prioritize investing and growing their money.

2. OVERCOMING LIMITING Beliefs About Money

Many people grow up believing myths such as "Money is the root of all evil" or "Rich people are greedy." These beliefs can block financial success. To change your financial future, you must:

Identify and challenge negative beliefs about money.

Replace them with empowering beliefs, such as "Money is a tool for creating a better life."

Surround yourself with people who have a success-oriented mindset.

3. DEVELOPING A GROWTH Mindset for Wealth

A fixed mindset assumes intelligence and ability are static, while a growth mindset believes that skills and knowledge can be developed. When it comes to wealth:

Understand that financial success is a skill that can be learned.

See failures as learning experiences rather than reasons to quit.

Continuously educate yourself through books, courses, and mentorships.

4. THE POWER OF GOAL Setting

Setting clear financial goals creates direction and motivation. Follow these steps:

Define Your Financial Goals – Do you want to save $10,000? Start a business? Achieve financial independence?

Break Goals Into Actionable Steps – Instead of saying, "I want to be rich," specify, "I will save $500 per month."

Visualize Success Daily – Imagine achieving your goals to build confidence and focus.

5. CREATING WEALTH-Oriented Habits

Wealthy people don't just think differently—they act differently. Develop these habits:

Save Before You Spend – Allocate a portion of your income to savings and investments before paying expenses.

Invest Consistently – Even small investments compound over time.

Expand Your Income Streams – Relying on one income source is risky; develop multiple streams.

Stay Disciplined and Persistent – Financial success takes time, but consistency pays off.

FINAL THOUGHTS

Adopting a mindset of financial success is the first and most crucial step in your wealth-building journey. The strategies and opportunities covered in later chapters will only be effective if you approach them with confidence, resilience, and a commitment to growth.

In the next chapter, we will dive into the fundamental principles of money and value—how money is created, how it flows in the economy, and how you can position yourself to benefit from its movement.

Chapter 2: Understanding Money & Value

The Role of Money in Society

Money is not just paper or digital numbers in a bank account; it represents value, trust, and the ability to exchange goods and services. To master earning money, you must first understand its role and significance in the economy.

1. The Evolution of Money

Barter System: Before money, people exchanged goods and services directly.

Commodity Money: Precious metals like gold and silver were used as early currency.

Paper Money & Banking: Governments introduced paper money backed by gold reserves.

Fiat Currency & Digital Transactions: Today's money is backed by trust in governments and financial institutions, with digital transactions dominating commerce.

2. HOW MONEY FLOWS in the Economy

Understanding the movement of money helps you position yourself to benefit from its circulation:

Production & Value Creation: Businesses and individuals create value through goods and services.

Earnings & Spending: Employees earn wages, and businesses generate revenue.

Investments & Wealth Growth: Smart investments allow money to multiply over time.

Government Influence: Policies, inflation, and interest rates affect money's purchasing power.

3. THE CONCEPT OF SUPPLY & Demand

Money follows opportunity. If you understand supply and demand, you can:

Identify profitable industries and trends.

Offer valuable skills or products where demand is high.

Price goods and services competitively to maximize profit.

4. THE IMPORTANCE OF Financial Literacy

Most financial struggles stem from a lack of knowledge about money management. Essential financial literacy skills include:

Budgeting: Tracking income and expenses to avoid unnecessary spending.

Debt Management: Using credit wisely and avoiding high-interest loans.

Investment Basics: Learning about stocks, real estate, and passive income sources.

Risk Assessment: Understanding and mitigating financial risks.

5. POSITIONING YOURSELF for Financial Success

To succeed financially, you must:

Continuously increase your earning potential through skills and education.

Recognize and seize opportunities in high-demand industries.

Manage and grow your money wisely through smart investments.
Adapt to economic changes and financial trends.

FINAL THOUGHTS

Understanding money and value is key to mastering wealth creation. Once you grasp how money flows and where opportunities exist, you can make strategic financial decisions to build long-term wealth.

In the next chapter, we will explore different types of income—active and passive—and how you can leverage both to achieve financial freedom.

Chapter 3: Active vs. Passive Income

Understanding Different Types of Income

To achieve financial success, you must understand the two primary ways to earn money: active and passive income. Knowing the differences and how to utilize both effectively is key to financial freedom.

1. WHAT IS ACTIVE INCOME?

Active income is money earned through direct effort and time. If you stop working, the income stops. Examples include:

Salary and Wages – Working a job and receiving a paycheck.

Freelancing – Getting paid for specific tasks like writing, design, or programming.

Consulting – Providing expertise to businesses or individuals for a fee.

Service-Based Business – Running a business where your time is exchanged for money (e.g., coaching, tutoring, repair services).

PROS OF ACTIVE INCOME:

Predictable and stable income source.

Easier to start earning quickly.

No large upfront investment required.

CONS OF ACTIVE INCOME:

Limited by time and effort.

No earnings if you stop working.

Can lead to burnout over time.

2. WHAT IS PASSIVE Income?

Passive income is money earned with little to no effort after the initial setup. It continues to generate earnings even when you are not actively working. Examples include:

Investments – Earning from stocks, bonds, or real estate.

Online Businesses – Selling digital products, courses, or automated services.

Affiliate Marketing – Promoting products and earning a commission.

Rental Properties – Owning real estate that generates rental income.

Royalties – Earning from books, music, or patented inventions.

PROS OF PASSIVE INCOME:

Can generate money while you sleep.

Provides financial security and long-term wealth.

Allows for financial independence.

CONS OF PASSIVE INCOME:

Often requires an initial investment of money or effort.

May take time to build consistent income.

Requires knowledge and strategic planning.

3. BALANCING ACTIVE and Passive Income

The most financially successful people create a mix of active and passive income sources. Here's how you can transition from relying solely on active income to building passive income streams:

Step 1: Maximize your active income – Use your job or freelance work to save and invest in passive income sources.

Step 2: Start a side hustle – Begin with something small, like an online store or affiliate marketing.

Step 3: Invest wisely – Put money into stocks, real estate, or other income-generating assets.

Step 4: Automate and scale – Once you have a working passive income stream, find ways to scale it.

FINAL THOUGHTS

Understanding the difference between active and passive income is crucial in your journey to financial independence. While active income is necessary for immediate survival, passive income is what ultimately provides financial freedom.

In the next chapter, we will explore how to build multiple streams of income so you're never reliant on a single source of earnings.

Chapter 4: Building Multiple Streams of Income

Why Multiple Streams of Income Matter

Relying on a single source of income can be risky. If that income disappears, you may face financial hardship. By diversifying and building multiple income streams, you create financial stability and open doors to wealth accumulation.

1. UNDERSTANDING THE Different Income Streams

There are various types of income streams you can build. Here are some of the most effective ones:

a. Earned Income (Active Income)

This is money earned by exchanging time and effort for wages or salary.

Example: Full-time job, freelancing, consulting.

B. BUSINESS INCOME

Owning a business allows you to generate money beyond your personal efforts.

Example: Selling products online, offering services, or creating an app.

C. INVESTMENT INCOME

Money made from financial investments that grow over time.

Example: Stocks, dividends, real estate, cryptocurrency.

D. PASSIVE INCOME

Income earned with minimal ongoing effort after initial setup.

Example: Affiliate marketing, royalties, automated digital businesses.

E. RENTAL INCOME

Owning property and renting it out for profit.

Example: Apartments, vacation rentals, commercial properties.

F. LICENSING AND ROYALTIES

Earning money from intellectual property rights.

Example: Publishing books, music royalties, patent licensing.

2. STEPS TO BUILDING Multiple Streams of Income

To successfully build multiple streams of income, follow these steps:

Step 1: Analyze Your Skills and Interests

Identify what you are good at and what you enjoy doing.

Consider monetizing hobbies, skills, or existing knowledge.

STEP 2: START WITH One Additional Income Stream

Don't overwhelm yourself. Begin with one additional source before adding more.

Example: If you have a full-time job, start a small online store or freelance.

STEP 3: AUTOMATE AND Scale

Use automation tools to manage side income with less effort.

Scale successful ventures by reinvesting profits or expanding services.

STEP 4: REINVEST EARNINGS

Use earnings from one stream to build another.

Example: Profits from a side business can be invested in stocks or rental property.

STEP 5: MONITOR AND Adjust

Track performance and make improvements.

If an income stream is not performing well, pivot or replace it.

3. COMMON MISTAKES to Avoid

Trying Too Many at Once – Focus on building one solid stream before diversifying further.

Lack of Research – Understand each opportunity before investing time or money.

Neglecting Active Income – Ensure your primary income source remains stable before shifting focus.

Not Reinventing or Scaling – Improve and expand successful income sources over time.

FINAL THOUGHTS

Building multiple income streams is essential for financial security and long-term wealth. By strategically incorporating different sources of income, you can create a more resilient financial future.

In the next chapter, we will discuss how to develop a profitable side hustle that complements your main income.

Chapter 5: How to Develop a Profitable Side Hustle

Why a Side Hustle Matters

A side hustle can provide extra income, financial security, and an opportunity to pursue your passions. Unlike traditional jobs, side hustles allow flexibility and can eventually grow into full-time businesses.

1. CHOOSING THE RIGHT Side Hustle

Before starting a side hustle, consider the following factors:

a. Your Skills and Interests

Identify what you enjoy doing and where your strengths lie.

Example: If you enjoy writing, consider freelance writing or blogging.

B. MARKET DEMAND

Research whether there is demand for your chosen side hustle.

Use tools like Google Trends, keyword research, and competitor analysis.

C. TIME COMMITMENT

Choose a side hustle that fits your schedule.

Example: If you work full-time, opt for a flexible, part-time gig like dropshipping or affiliate marketing.

D. PROFITABILITY POTENTIAL

Assess how much you can realistically earn.

Calculate startup costs, expected revenue, and profit margins.

2. POPULAR SIDE HUSTLE Ideas

There are many side hustles to choose from. Here are some profitable options:

a. Online Side Hustles

Freelance writing, graphic design, and programming.

Selling digital products (eBooks, courses, printables).

Dropshipping and eCommerce.

Affiliate marketing and blogging.

B. SERVICE-BASED SIDE Hustles

Tutoring or coaching (academic, fitness, career advice).

Photography and videography.

House cleaning or pet sitting.

C. INVESTMENT-BASED Side Hustles

Stock trading or cryptocurrency investing.

Real estate rentals.

Peer-to-peer lending.

3. SETTING UP YOUR Side Hustle for Success

To ensure your side hustle thrives, follow these key steps:

Step 1: Create a Simple Business Plan

Outline your goals, budget, and strategies.

Identify your target audience and competition.

STEP 2: BUILD AN ONLINE Presence

Create a website or social media pages.

Showcase your portfolio and expertise.

STEP 3: SET REALISTIC Goals and Milestones

Establish short-term and long-term targets.

Track progress using financial and performance metrics.

STEP 4: MANAGE YOUR Time Wisely

Use productivity tools like calendars and task managers.

Dedicate specific hours to your side hustle.

STEP 5: SCALE YOUR Side Hustle

Automate repetitive tasks.

Reinvest profits into marketing and expansion.

Consider outsourcing as your business grows.

4. AVOIDING COMMON Side Hustle Pitfalls

Lack of Consistency – Treat your side hustle like a business, not a hobby.

Ignoring Customer Feedback – Adapt based on market demands.

Poor Financial Management – Keep track of expenses and reinvest wisely.

Burnout – Maintain a balance between your job, side hustle, and personal life.

FINAL THOUGHTS

A successful side hustle requires dedication, smart planning, and continuous learning. If done correctly, it can supplement your income and even become your main source of revenue.

In the next chapter, we will explore how to transition from a side hustle to a full-time business.

Chapter 6: Transitioning from Side Hustle to Full-Time Business

Why Transitioning Matters

If your side hustle is generating consistent income and growth, it may be time to consider making it your primary source of income. However, transitioning requires careful planning to ensure financial stability and long-term success.

1. IDENTIFYING THE Right Time to Transition

Before quitting your job, assess whether your side hustle is ready for full-time commitment.

a. Financial Readiness

Ensure your side hustle earns enough to cover your living expenses.

Save at least 3-6 months' worth of expenses as a safety net.

B. CONSISTENT REVENUE Stream

Your side hustle should have steady and predictable income.

Review income trends to ensure sustainability.

C. DEMAND AND GROWTH Potential

If demand is increasing, it may be time to scale up.

Analyze market trends and customer feedback.

2. PLANNING YOUR EXIT Strategy

Leaving a full-time job requires a well-thought-out plan.

Step 1: Set Clear Goals and Milestones

Define income targets before quitting your job.

Plan growth strategies to scale the business.

STEP 2: CREATE A BUSINESS Budget

Track expenses and separate personal and business finances.

Set aside money for taxes, reinvestment, and emergencies.

STEP 3: BUILD A STRONG Client Base

Secure long-term clients or recurring revenue sources.

Strengthen customer relationships to ensure steady sales.

STEP 4: AUTOMATE AND Delegate Tasks

Use automation tools to streamline operations.

Hire freelancers or employees as needed.

STEP 5: TEST YOUR TRANSITION

Try working part-time before fully committing.

Gradually reduce your job hours while growing your business.

3. OVERCOMING CHALLENGES in Transitioning

Fear of Uncertainty – Financial insecurity can be daunting. Keep a financial cushion and multiple income streams.

Managing Workload – Prioritize essential tasks and set clear work hours.

Scaling Too Fast – Grow at a sustainable pace to avoid financial strain.

Isolation & Burnout – Join entrepreneur communities for support and guidance.

4. FINAL STEPS TO FULL-Time Entrepreneurship

Register your business legally and obtain necessary licenses.

Improve branding and marketing to attract more clients.

Continuously learn and adapt to market changes.

FINAL THOUGHTS

Transitioning from a side hustle to a full-time business is a significant milestone. With strategic planning, financial preparedness, and a growth mindset, you can successfully make the leap and enjoy the benefits of being your own boss.

In the next chapter, we will explore effective marketing strategies to grow your business and attract more customers.

Chapter 7: Marketing Strategies for Business Growth

Why Marketing is Essential

Marketing is the backbone of any successful business. Without effective marketing strategies, even the best products or services may struggle to gain visibility and attract customers. This chapter explores proven marketing techniques to grow your business.

1. UNDERSTANDING YOUR Target Audience

Before marketing, you must identify your ideal customers.

a. Define Your Target Market

Identify demographics (age, gender, income, location).

Understand customer pain points and needs.

B. CREATE CUSTOMER Personas

Develop fictional profiles representing your ideal clients.

Personalize your marketing messages to their interests.

C. ANALYZE COMPETITORS

Study competitors' marketing strategies.

Identify gaps in the market and differentiate yourself.

2. BUILDING AN EFFECTIVE Marketing Plan

An organized marketing plan helps in achieving growth goals.

Step 1: Set Clear Marketing Goals

Increase brand awareness, website traffic, or sales.

Use SMART (Specific, Measurable, Achievable, Relevant, Time-bound) objectives.

STEP 2: CHOOSE THE Right Marketing Channels

Social Media (Facebook, Instagram, LinkedIn, Twitter)

Content Marketing (Blogs, Videos, Podcasts)

Email Marketing (Newsletters, Promotions)

Paid Advertising (Google Ads, Facebook Ads)

Influencer Partnerships (Collaboration with niche influencers)

STEP 3: ALLOCATE A Marketing Budget

Determine how much to invest in different channels.

Prioritize cost-effective strategies with high ROI.

3. DIGITAL MARKETING Strategies

a. Social Media Marketing

Post regularly and engage with your audience.

Use visually appealing content (images, videos, infographics).

Leverage hashtags and trends for more visibility.

B. CONTENT MARKETING

Write blogs and articles that solve customer problems.

Create engaging videos and educational content.

Optimize content for search engines (SEO).

C. EMAIL MARKETING

Build an email list of potential customers.

Send personalized offers and updates.

Automate email sequences for consistent engagement.

D. PAID ADVERTISING

Run targeted ads to reach potential customers.

A/B test different ads to improve performance.

Monitor metrics and adjust strategies accordingly.

4. OFFLINE MARKETING Strategies

Networking and attending industry events.

Distributing flyers and promotional materials.

Word-of-mouth referrals and customer incentives.

5. MEASURING MARKETING Success

Tracking and analyzing marketing efforts ensures continuous improvement.

Use Google Analytics to track website traffic.

Monitor engagement metrics on social media.

Adjust campaigns based on performance data.

FINAL THOUGHTS

A strong marketing strategy fuels business growth and customer engagement. Consistency, creativity, and adaptability are key to long-term success.

In the next chapter, we will explore how to build a strong brand identity that resonates with your audience.

Chapter 8: Building a Strong Brand Identity

Why Branding Matters

A strong brand identity sets your business apart and builds customer trust. It influences how people perceive your business and creates lasting impressions. This chapter will guide you in developing a unique and impactful brand identity.

1. UNDERSTANDING BRAND Identity

Brand identity encompasses all the visual and emotional elements that represent your business.

a. Key Elements of a Strong Brand Identity

Brand Name: A memorable and relevant name.

Logo: A visually appealing symbol that represents your business.

Color Scheme: Colors that evoke emotions and align with your industry.

Typography: Fonts that reflect your brand's personality.

Brand Voice: The tone and style of communication.

Slogan/Tagline: A short and impactful phrase that conveys your brand's essence.

B. THE ROLE OF BRANDING in Business Success

Increases recognition and customer loyalty.

Creates trust and credibility in the market.
Helps differentiate from competitors.

2. DEFINING YOUR BRAND Identity

Step 1: Establish Your Brand Mission & Values
Define your business's purpose and core beliefs.
Ensure they align with customer expectations.

STEP 2: IDENTIFY YOUR Target Audience

Understand who your customers are and what they value.
Tailor branding elements to appeal to your ideal audience.

STEP 3: CRAFT YOUR Brand Personality

Decide whether your brand is formal, friendly, innovative, or traditional.

Align branding with your brand's tone and voice.

STEP 4: DESIGN A MEMORABLE Logo and Visual Identity

Work with a designer or use online tools to create a professional logo.

Maintain a consistent color palette and typography across all materials.

3. ESTABLISHING BRAND Consistency

Consistency strengthens brand recognition and trust.

Use the same colors, fonts, and logo across all platforms.

Maintain a consistent tone of voice in marketing and communication.

Ensure all customer interactions reflect your brand values.

4. BUILDING BRAND AWARENESS

Increase visibility and reach a wider audience through various strategies.

Leverage social media to showcase your brand identity.

Collaborate with influencers and brand ambassadors.

Create high-quality content that reflects your brand values.

Use storytelling to connect emotionally with your audience.

5. EVOLVING YOUR BRAND Over Time

As your business grows, your brand identity may need updates.

Stay adaptable to market trends and customer preferences.

Rebrand strategically if your business undergoes significant changes.

Keep your brand fresh while maintaining its core essence.

FINAL THOUGHTS

A well-defined brand identity is crucial for long-term success. By consistently presenting a strong and authentic brand, you can build customer loyalty and distinguish yourself in the market.

In the next chapter, we will explore customer relationship management and how to maintain strong connections with your audience.

Chapter 9: Customer Relationship Management

Why Customer Relationships Matter

Strong customer relationships lead to loyalty, repeat business, and positive word-of-mouth marketing. Managing these relationships effectively can significantly impact business growth and profitability. This chapter explores strategies to build and maintain strong customer connections.

1. UNDERSTANDING CUSTOMER Relationship Management (CRM)

CRM is the process of managing interactions with current and potential customers to improve relationships and drive sales.

a. Benefits of CRM

Enhances customer satisfaction and retention.

Helps understand customer needs and preferences.

Increases sales through personalized marketing.

Streamlines customer support and communication.

B. TYPES OF CRM SYSTEMS

Operational CRM: Focuses on sales, marketing, and service automation.

Analytical CRM: Uses data analysis to improve customer relationships.

Collaborative CRM: Enhances communication between different departments for a seamless customer experience.

2. STRATEGIES FOR BUILDING Strong Customer Relationships

Step 1: Provide Excellent Customer Service

Respond promptly to inquiries and complaints.

Offer personalized support to make customers feel valued.

STEP 2: COMMUNICATE Effectively

Use multiple channels (email, chat, phone, social media) for customer engagement.

Send regular updates, promotions, and personalized messages.

STEP 3: REWARD LOYALTY

Implement loyalty programs, discounts, or special offers for returning customers.

Recognize and appreciate long-term customers through exclusive perks.

STEP 4: GATHER AND Utilize Customer Feedback

Conduct surveys and collect reviews to understand customer expectations.

Improve products and services based on customer insights.

STEP 5: USE CRM SOFTWARE for Better Management

Automate follow-ups and customer interactions.

Track customer history and preferences for personalized experiences.

3. HANDLING CUSTOMER Complaints and Conflict Resolution

Handling complaints professionally can turn a dissatisfied customer into a loyal one.

Listen actively and empathize with the customer.

Apologize and offer a solution promptly.

Follow up to ensure the issue is fully resolved.

4. SCALING CUSTOMER Relationship Management as Your Business Grows

Invest in advanced CRM tools to handle increasing customer interactions.

Train employees to maintain high standards of customer service.

Continuously adapt strategies to evolving customer needs and expectations.

FINAL THOUGHTS

Effective customer relationship management fosters trust, satisfaction, and long-term business success. By prioritizing customer needs and leveraging CRM tools, you can create lasting relationships that drive growth.

In the next chapter, we will explore financial management strategies to ensure business stability and profitability.

Chapter 10: Financial Management for Entrepreneurs

Why Financial Management Matters

Effective financial management is crucial for business sustainability and growth. Properly managing finances ensures stability, allows for strategic investments, and helps entrepreneurs avoid financial pitfalls. This chapter covers key principles and strategies for financial success.

1. UNDERSTANDING BUSINESS Finances

Financial literacy is essential for making informed decisions.

a. Key Financial Statements

Income Statement: Shows revenue, expenses, and profits over a period.

Balance Sheet: Provides a snapshot of assets, liabilities, and equity.

Cash Flow Statement: Tracks money flowing in and out of the business.

B. IMPORTANCE OF BUDGETING

Helps control expenses and allocate resources efficiently.

Prevents overspending and financial mismanagement.

Provides a clear financial roadmap for growth.

2. MANAGING CASH FLOW

Cash flow is the lifeblood of a business. Managing it effectively ensures operational stability.

Step 1: Monitor Income and Expenses

Track all financial transactions regularly.

Use accounting software to maintain accurate records.

STEP 2: MAINTAIN A Cash Reserve

Save for emergencies and unexpected expenses.

Keep at least three to six months' worth of expenses in reserve.

STEP 3: OPTIMIZE PAYMENT Cycles

Negotiate better payment terms with suppliers.

Encourage prompt payments from customers.

3. COST MANAGEMENT and Profitability

Reducing unnecessary costs and increasing profitability ensures long-term business success.

Identify and cut unnecessary expenses.

Invest in cost-effective marketing and operational strategies.

Improve pricing strategies to maximize profits.

4. FUNDING AND INVESTMENT Strategies

Entrepreneurs may need funding to grow their businesses. Understanding financing options is crucial.

a. Types of Business Funding

Bootstrapping: Using personal savings or business revenue.

Loans: Bank loans or government grants.

Investors: Seeking funding from angel investors or venture capitalists.

Crowdfunding: Raising money from multiple small investors online.

B. WHEN TO SEEK INVESTMENT

If expanding operations requires significant capital.

When launching a new product or entering new markets.

If cash flow constraints hinder growth.

5. TAX PLANNING AND Compliance

Understanding tax obligations helps avoid legal issues and financial penalties.

Keep accurate financial records for tax reporting.

Take advantage of tax deductions and incentives.

Consult a tax professional for compliance and efficiency.

FINAL THOUGHTS

Strong financial management is key to sustaining and scaling a business. Entrepreneurs who master budgeting, cash flow management, and investment strategies position themselves for long-term success.

In the next chapter, we will explore business expansion strategies and scaling operations effectively.

Chapter 11: Scaling Your Business

Why Scaling Matters

Scaling a business involves increasing revenue while managing costs efficiently. Growth should be strategic, ensuring that operations, customer service, and financial stability remain strong. This chapter covers essential strategies to scale your business effectively.

1. PREPARING FOR BUSINESS Growth

Scaling requires a strong foundation. Evaluate your business to ensure it's ready for expansion.

a. Assessing Business Readiness

Is demand for your product/service increasing?

Do you have a strong financial foundation?

Can your team and systems handle growth?

B. SETTING CLEAR GROWTH Goals

Define short-term and long-term expansion objectives.

Set key performance indicators (KPIs) to track progress.

2. EXPANDING OPERATIONS Efficiently

Step 1: Streamline Processes

Automate repetitive tasks to improve efficiency.

Implement scalable technology solutions.

STEP 2: OPTIMIZE SUPPLY Chain Management

Negotiate better deals with suppliers.

Ensure inventory management supports growth.

STEP 3: STRENGTHEN Team and Leadership

Hire skilled employees to manage increased workload.

Develop leadership training programs.

3. DIVERSIFYING REVENUE Streams

Reducing dependency on a single income source ensures long-term stability.

Introduce new products or services to complement existing offerings.

Explore partnerships and collaborations.

Expand into new geographic markets or online platforms.

4. LEVERAGING MARKETING and Branding for Growth

a. Strengthening Online Presence

Invest in digital marketing and SEO.

Use data-driven marketing strategies.

B. EXPANDING CUSTOMER Acquisition Strategies

Implement referral programs to attract new customers.

Develop loyalty programs to retain existing clients.

5. MANAGING FINANCIAL Risks in Scaling

Growth must be financially sustainable. Avoid cash flow issues by:

Forecasting financial needs before scaling.

Securing funding options like business loans or investor capital.

Monitoring expenses and adjusting strategies accordingly.

FINAL THOUGHTS

Scaling a business requires strategic planning, financial management, and operational efficiency. By preparing for growth, optimizing operations, and diversifying revenue, businesses can scale sustainably and successfully.

In the next chapter, we will explore how to expand your team and build a strong workforce to support business growth.

Chapter 12: Building a High-Performing Team

Why a Strong Team Matters

A business is only as strong as its team. A high-performing team drives efficiency, innovation, and long-term success. This chapter explores strategies for hiring, training, and managing a successful workforce.

1. HIRING THE RIGHT People

Recruitment is the foundation of a great team. Hiring the right employees ensures productivity and a positive work culture.

a. Defining Job Roles Clearly

Create detailed job descriptions with clear responsibilities.

Set qualifications and expectations to attract the right candidates.

B. EFFECTIVE HIRING Strategies

Use multiple channels (job boards, referrals, networking) to find talent.

Conduct structured interviews to assess skills and cultural fit.

C. ONBOARDING AND TRAINING

Provide thorough orientation to integrate new hires smoothly.

Offer mentorship programs and training sessions to accelerate learning.

2. BUILDING A POSITIVE Work Culture

A strong team culture enhances motivation and retention.

Step 1: Foster Open Communication

Encourage transparency and feedback within the team.

Use team meetings and one-on-one check-ins to maintain alignment.

STEP 2: PROMOTE COLLABORATION and Teamwork

Organize team-building activities and group projects.

Reward collaboration to strengthen team dynamics.

STEP 3: RECOGNIZE AND Reward Performance

Implement an employee recognition program.

Offer performance-based incentives to boost morale.

3. LEADERSHIP AND MANAGEMENT Best Practices

Strong leadership ensures a high-performing team stays motivated and productive.

Lead by example and demonstrate integrity.

Set clear goals and provide constructive feedback.

Empower employees by giving them autonomy and growth opportunities.

4. RETAINING TOP TALENT

Keeping skilled employees reduces hiring costs and strengthens the business.

Offer career growth opportunities and continuous learning.

Provide competitive salaries and benefits.

Create a supportive and inclusive work environment.

FINAL THOUGHTS

A strong, motivated team is essential for business growth. By hiring the right people, fostering a positive culture, and implementing effective leadership strategies, businesses can build a workforce that drives long-term success.

In the next chapter, we will explore the importance of innovation and staying competitive in the marketplace.

Chapter 13: Innovation and Staying Competitive

Why Innovation Matters

In a fast-changing business environment, innovation is key to staying ahead of the competition. Businesses that continuously evolve and improve their products, services, and processes have a higher chance of long-term success.

1. UNDERSTANDING MARKET Trends

Keeping up with trends allows businesses to adapt and innovate effectively.

a. Researching Industry Developments

Follow market reports and industry publications.

Attend conferences and networking events to gain insights.

B. ANALYZING COMPETITOR Strategies

Study competitors to identify their strengths and weaknesses.

Learn from their successes and mistakes to refine your approach.

C. LISTENING TO CUSTOMER Needs

Conduct surveys and feedback sessions.

Use customer insights to improve products and services.

2. ENCOURAGING A CULTURE of Innovation

Fostering creativity within your business encourages fresh ideas and improvements.

Step 1: Empower Employees to Innovate

Encourage employees to share ideas and experiment with solutions.

Provide an open environment for creative discussions.

STEP 2: INVEST IN RESEARCH and Development (R&D)

Allocate resources to test new concepts and refine existing offerings.

Partner with experts or institutions for cutting-edge insights.

STEP 3: UTILIZE TECHNOLOGY for Growth

Implement new tools and automation to improve efficiency.

Stay updated with advancements like artificial intelligence, big data, and digital marketing.

3. ADAPTING TO CHANGING Consumer Behavior

Understanding consumer preferences and adapting quickly keeps businesses relevant.

Monitor shifts in consumer behavior using analytics and feedback.

Personalize marketing and product offerings to match customer expectations.

Leverage digital platforms to engage with a wider audience.

4. STRATEGIC RISK-TAKING

Innovation often involves taking calculated risks. Smart decision-making can lead to breakthrough success.

Test new ideas on a small scale before full implementation.

Learn from failures and adjust strategies accordingly.

Stay flexible and open to pivoting when needed.

FINAL THOUGHTS

Innovation is the key to staying competitive in a dynamic marketplace. By staying informed, fostering creativity, and adapting to changes, businesses can continue to thrive and grow.

In the next chapter, we will explore the power of networking and business partnerships to further enhance opportunities and success.

Chapter 14: Networking and Business Partnerships

Why Networking Matters

Building strong professional relationships can open doors to new opportunities, partnerships, and business growth. Successful networking allows entrepreneurs to gain valuable insights, collaborate with others, and access new markets.

1. THE POWER OF NETWORKING

a. Expanding Your Professional Circle

Join industry groups, business associations, and networking events.

Use social media platforms like LinkedIn to connect with professionals.

B. BUILDING MEANINGFUL Relationships

Focus on creating genuine connections rather than just seeking favors.

Offer value to others by sharing knowledge, resources, or referrals.

C. LEVERAGING YOUR Network for Growth

Seek mentorship from experienced professionals.

Collaborate on projects or joint ventures for mutual benefit.

2. ESTABLISHING STRONG Business Partnerships

Strategic partnerships can enhance resources, credibility, and market reach.

Step 1: Identifying Potential Partners

Look for businesses that complement rather than compete with yours.

Evaluate shared goals, values, and long-term compatibility.

STEP 2: CREATING WIN-Win Collaborations

Develop agreements that benefit both parties.

Set clear expectations, roles, and responsibilities.

STEP 3: MAINTAINING Strong Partnerships

Communicate openly and regularly with partners.

Address challenges collaboratively and adjust strategies as needed.

3. MAKING THE MOST of Networking Events

Attending events is an effective way to meet new people and expand your network.

Prepare an elevator pitch to introduce yourself concisely.

Engage in meaningful conversations rather than making quick sales pitches.

Follow up with new contacts to build lasting relationships.

4. ONLINE NETWORKING and Digital Collaboration

With digital tools, networking is no longer limited to in-person events.

Participate in online forums, webinars, and virtual conferences.

Use email and social media to maintain professional connections.

Leverage online platforms to collaborate with remote partners.

FINAL THOUGHTS

Effective networking and strategic partnerships can accelerate business growth and create valuable opportunities. By building strong professional relationships, entrepreneurs can gain access to resources, support, and new markets.

In the next chapter, we will discuss the role of customer relationship management (CRM) and how it can enhance business success.

Chapter 15: Customer Relationship Management (CRM) Strategies

Why CRM Matters

Customer Relationship Management (CRM) is essential for building long-term relationships, enhancing customer satisfaction, and increasing business revenue. A well-implemented CRM strategy allows businesses to understand and meet customer needs effectively.

1. UNDERSTANDING CRM and Its Importance

a. What is CRM?

CRM refers to strategies, technologies, and practices used to manage customer interactions.

It helps track customer preferences, behavior, and history to enhance service quality.

B. BENEFITS OF CRM

Improves customer retention and loyalty.

Increases sales through personalized engagement.

Streamlines business processes and enhances efficiency.

2. CHOOSING THE RIGHT CRM System

Selecting a CRM system that aligns with your business needs is crucial.

Step 1: Identify Your Business Requirements

Determine the features you need, such as automation, analytics, and integration with other tools.

Consider the size and complexity of your customer base.

STEP 2: COMPARE CRM Software Options

Popular CRM tools include Salesforce, HubSpot, and Zoho CRM.

Evaluate cost, user-friendliness, and scalability.

STEP 3: IMPLEMENT AND Train Your Team

Ensure smooth integration with existing systems.

Provide training to employees for optimal usage.

3. BUILDING STRONG Customer Relationships

A CRM strategy should focus on creating personalized and meaningful interactions.

Use customer data to tailor marketing and communication efforts.

Send follow-up emails, birthday messages, and personalized offers.

Respond promptly to inquiries and provide excellent customer support.

4. MEASURING CRM SUCCESS

To maximize CRM benefits, track key performance indicators (KPIs).

Monitor customer satisfaction and retention rates.

Analyze sales growth and conversion rates.

Use CRM analytics to refine strategies and improve engagement.

FINAL THOUGHTS

A well-executed CRM strategy strengthens customer loyalty and drives business growth. By leveraging CRM tools and fostering personalized interactions, businesses can build lasting relationships and maximize customer satisfaction.

In the next chapter, we will explore effective digital marketing strategies to boost brand visibility and engagement.

Chapter 16: Digital Marketing Strategies

Why Digital Marketing Matters

Digital marketing is essential for reaching a larger audience, building brand awareness, and driving sales. With the rise of online platforms, businesses must adopt effective digital strategies to stay competitive.

1. UNDERSTANDING DIGITAL Marketing Channels

a. Social Media Marketing

Platforms like Facebook, Instagram, Twitter, and LinkedIn help businesses engage with customers.

Create compelling content, run ads, and interact with followers to build brand loyalty.

B. SEARCH ENGINE OPTIMIZATION (SEO)

Optimize website content to rank higher on search engines.

Use relevant keywords, high-quality backlinks, and proper meta tags.

C. EMAIL MARKETING

Build an email list and send personalized offers, newsletters, and promotions.

Use automation tools to nurture leads and retain customers.

D. CONTENT MARKETING

Publish blog posts, videos, and infographics to attract and educate customers.

Focus on providing value rather than direct selling.

E. PAY-PER-CLICK (PPC) Advertising

Platforms like Google Ads allow businesses to run targeted ad campaigns.

Control budget and measure performance through analytics.

2. CREATING AN EFFECTIVE Digital Marketing Strategy

Step 1: Define Your Goals

Set clear objectives such as increasing website traffic, generating leads, or boosting sales.

STEP 2: IDENTIFY YOUR Target Audience

Conduct market research to understand customer demographics and preferences.

STEP 3: DEVELOP A CONTENT Plan

Create a content calendar with planned topics and posting schedules.

STEP 4: UTILIZE DATA Analytics

Track marketing performance using tools like Google Analytics and social media insights.

Adjust strategies based on data-driven decisions.

3. ENGAGING WITH CUSTOMERS Online

Respond to comments and messages promptly.

Host live sessions, Q&A, and giveaways to boost engagement.

Encourage user-generated content and reviews.

4. MEASURING SUCCESS and Adjusting Strategies

Monitor key performance indicators (KPIs) such as website traffic, conversion rates, and engagement metrics.

Experiment with A/B testing to optimize marketing campaigns.

Stay updated with the latest digital marketing trends.

FINAL THOUGHTS

Digital marketing is a powerful tool for business growth. By leveraging the right channels and strategies, businesses can attract, engage, and convert potential customers effectively.

In the next chapter, we will explore financial management strategies to help businesses maintain profitability and sustainability.

Chapter 17: Financial Management for Business Success

Why Financial Management Matters

Effective financial management is crucial for maintaining profitability, ensuring sustainability, and making informed business decisions. Understanding financial principles helps businesses allocate resources efficiently and achieve long-term success.

1. KEY FINANCIAL PRINCIPLES for Businesses

a. Budgeting and Expense Control

Develop a realistic budget that aligns with business goals.

Track expenses and identify areas for cost reduction.

B. REVENUE MANAGEMENT

Diversify income streams to reduce financial risks.

Focus on pricing strategies that maximize profit margins.

C. CASH FLOW MANAGEMENT

Monitor cash inflows and outflows to maintain liquidity.

Avoid excessive debt and ensure timely payments to suppliers.

2. FINANCIAL PLANNING and Forecasting

Step 1: Set Financial Goals

Establish short-term and long-term financial objectives.

Align financial goals with business growth strategies.

STEP 2: ANALYZE FINANCIAL Statements

Review balance sheets, income statements, and cash flow reports.

Identify financial trends and areas for improvement.

STEP 3: USE FINANCIAL Tools and Software

Leverage accounting software like QuickBooks or FreshBooks.

Automate financial processes for better accuracy and efficiency.

3. MANAGING BUSINESS Investments

Evaluate investment opportunities based on risk and return.

Allocate funds to high-impact areas such as marketing and innovation.

Monitor investment performance regularly.

4. TAX PLANNING AND Compliance

Stay informed about tax regulations and deadlines.

Work with a financial advisor or accountant to optimize tax strategies.

Take advantage of deductions and credits to minimize tax liability.

5. SECURING BUSINESS Financing

Explore funding options like bank loans, venture capital, and crowdfunding.

Maintain a strong credit score to increase loan approval chances.

Present a solid business plan when seeking financial backing.

FINAL THOUGHTS

Sound financial management is essential for business growth and stability. By implementing effective budgeting, cash flow monitoring, and investment strategies, businesses can achieve long-term success.

In the next chapter, we will discuss strategies for scaling and expanding your business to reach new heights.

Chapter 18: Scaling and Expanding Your Business

Why Business Expansion Matters

Scaling a business is essential for increasing revenue, market presence, and long-term success. Understanding the right strategies for expansion helps minimize risks and maximize growth opportunities.

1. IDENTIFYING THE Right Time to Scale

a. Signs Your Business is Ready for Expansion

Consistent and increasing revenue streams.

Strong customer demand and brand recognition.

Efficient operational processes and stable infrastructure.

B. COMMON CHALLENGES in Scaling

Managing increased operational costs.

Maintaining product or service quality.

Ensuring sufficient workforce and resources.

2. STRATEGIES FOR BUSINESS Growth

Step 1: Market Research and Analysis

Identify new target audiences and market trends.

Conduct competitor analysis to position your business strategically.

STEP 2: EXPANDING PRODUCT or Service Offerings

Develop new products or enhance existing ones.

Diversify services to meet evolving customer needs.

STEP 3: STRENGTHENING Online and Offline Presence

Optimize digital marketing efforts through SEO, PPC, and social media.

Expand to new physical locations or distribution channels.

3. BUILDING A SCALABLE Business Model

Automate processes to enhance efficiency and reduce costs.

Implement scalable technology and customer management systems.

Establish partnerships or collaborations to extend market reach.

4. FINANCIAL PLANNING for Expansion

Secure additional funding through investors, business loans, or crowdfunding.

Create a detailed financial forecast to plan for growth-related expenses.

Manage risks by having contingency plans in place.

5. HIRING AND MANAGING a Growing Team

Recruit skilled professionals who align with your business vision.

Foster a positive workplace culture to retain employees.

Provide training and development programs to enhance team capabilities.

FINAL THOUGHTS

Scaling and expanding a business requires careful planning and execution. By implementing strategic growth initiatives, businesses can achieve sustainable success and increased profitability.

In the next chapter, we will explore the importance of building strong business networks and partnerships to fuel growth.

Chapter 19: Building Business Networks and Partnerships

Why Business Networking Matters

Building strong business networks and partnerships is essential for growth, resource sharing, and market expansion. Connections with other professionals can lead to new opportunities, collaborations, and long-term success.

1. UNDERSTANDING BUSINESS Networking

a. Benefits of Networking

Access to new clients, suppliers, and investors.

Opportunities for mentorship and knowledge exchange.

Increased brand visibility and credibility.

B. TYPES OF BUSINESS Networks

Industry-specific networks and trade associations.

Local business groups and chambers of commerce.

Online communities and professional social media platforms.

2. STRATEGIES FOR EFFECTIVE Networking

Step 1: Attend Events and Conferences

Participate in industry expos, trade shows, and business summits.

Engage in meaningful conversations and exchange contact information.

STEP 2: LEVERAGE SOCIAL Media and Online Platforms

Join LinkedIn groups and engage in discussions.

Use platforms like Twitter and Facebook to connect with professionals.

STEP 3: BUILD GENUINE Relationships

Focus on long-term connections rather than immediate gains.

Offer value by sharing insights, referrals, and resources.

3. FORMING STRATEGIC Partnerships

Identify businesses with complementary services or products.

Establish clear goals and mutual benefits for the partnership.

Create formal agreements to define responsibilities and expectations.

4. NURTURING AND MAINTAINING Relationships

Follow up with contacts regularly through emails or meetings.

Show appreciation by acknowledging partnerships and collaborations.

Stay engaged and offer help when possible to strengthen connections.

5. MEASURING THE IMPACT of Networking

Track the number of new leads, referrals, and partnerships gained.

Evaluate the effectiveness of networking events and online engagement.

Adjust networking strategies based on outcomes and feedback.

FINAL THOUGHTS

Successful business networking and partnerships open doors to growth and innovation. By actively engaging with the right connections and forming valuable collaborations, businesses can gain a competitive edge.

In the next chapter, we will explore how to enhance customer relationships and build a loyal client base.

Chapter 20: Enhancing Customer Relationships and Retention

Why Customer Relationships Matter

Strong customer relationships are key to business success. Retaining customers is often more cost-effective than acquiring new ones, and loyal customers can become brand advocates who drive referrals.

1. UNDERSTANDING CUSTOMER Needs

a. Importance of Customer Satisfaction

Happy customers are more likely to return and recommend your business.

Customer satisfaction directly impacts brand reputation and growth.

B. METHODS TO UNDERSTAND Customers

Conduct surveys and request feedback.

Monitor customer interactions and analyze purchasing behaviors.

2. BUILDING STRONG Customer Relationships

Step 1: Personalize Customer Interactions

Use customers' names and reference past interactions.

Tailor recommendations based on customer preferences.

STEP 2: PROVIDE EXCEPTIONAL Customer Service

Train staff to handle customer inquiries with professionalism and empathy.

Respond promptly to issues and go above and beyond to resolve concerns.

STEP 3: IMPLEMENT LOYALTY Programs

Offer discounts, rewards, or exclusive deals to repeat customers.

Create VIP programs to encourage long-term engagement.

3. LEVERAGING TECHNOLOGY for Customer Engagement

Use CRM (Customer Relationship Management) tools to track interactions.

Automate communication through chatbots and email marketing.

Engage customers through social media and personalized messaging.

4. HANDLING CUSTOMER Complaints Effectively

Listen actively and acknowledge customer concerns.

Apologize sincerely and offer fair solutions.

Follow up to ensure customer satisfaction post-resolution.

5. MEASURING CUSTOMER Retention and Loyalty

Track repeat purchases and customer lifetime value.
Analyze Net Promoter Score (NPS) to measure satisfaction.
Adjust strategies based on retention metrics and feedback.

FINAL THOUGHTS

Strong customer relationships lead to long-term success. By prioritizing personalized service, leveraging technology, and addressing concerns proactively, businesses can enhance customer loyalty and retention.

In the next chapter, we will explore strategies for effective sales and negotiation techniques to boost revenue.

Chapter 21: Sales and Negotiation Strategies for Growth

Why Sales and Negotiation Matter

Mastering sales and negotiation skills is crucial for business success. Effective selling and deal-making can lead to increased revenue, stronger client relationships, and long-term partnerships.

1. UNDERSTANDING THE Sales Process

a. The Stages of a Successful Sale

Prospecting: Identifying potential customers.

Approach: Making first contact and building rapport.

Presentation: Demonstrating the value of your product or service.

Handling Objections: Addressing concerns and hesitations.

Closing: Finalizing the deal and confirming the sale.

Follow-Up: Maintaining post-sale communication and satisfaction.

B. COMMON SALES MISTAKES to Avoid

Focusing too much on the product rather than customer needs.

Failing to listen and understand the client's concerns.

Not following up after the initial sale.

2. DEVELOPING PERSUASIVE Sales Techniques

Step 1: Build Trust and Credibility

Be transparent and honest about your offerings.

Show expertise in your industry and provide value upfront.

STEP 2: USE THE ART of Storytelling

Share success stories and customer testimonials.

Frame your product as the solution to a problem.

STEP 3: EMPLOY EFFECTIVE Closing Strategies

The Assumptive Close: Act as if the customer has already decided.

The Urgency Close: Highlight limited-time offers.

The Trial Close: Ask questions to gauge interest before the final close.

3. MASTERING NEGOTIATION for Win-Win Deals

Prepare Thoroughly: Understand client needs and possible objections.

Stay Confident, Yet Flexible: Aim for a favorable outcome but be willing to compromise.

Use Silence Effectively: Let the other party speak and reveal their priorities.

Know When to Walk Away: Recognize when a deal is not in your best interest.

4. LEVERAGING TECHNOLOGY in Sales

Use CRM tools to track leads and customer interactions.

Automate follow-ups through email and messaging systems.

Utilize data analytics to refine sales strategies.

5. MEASURING SALES Performance

Track conversion rates and deal closure ratios.

Analyze customer feedback to improve the sales approach.

Set realistic sales goals and adjust strategies accordingly.

FINAL THOUGHTS

Sales and negotiation skills are essential for business growth. By developing a structured sales process, employing persuasive techniques, and mastering negotiation, businesses can boost revenue and build lasting client relationships.

In the next chapter, we will explore digital marketing strategies to attract and retain customers.

Chapter 22: Mastering Digital Marketing for Maximum Profits

Why Digital Marketing Matters?

In today's digital age, online marketing is essential for business growth. Leveraging the power of the internet can significantly increase sales, reach, and brand recognition.

1. THE KEY ELEMENTS of Digital Marketing

Search Engine Optimization (SEO): Improving website visibility on Google.

Social Media Marketing: Engaging with customers on platforms like Facebook, Instagram, and LinkedIn.

Email Marketing: Nurturing leads and maintaining customer relationships.

Paid Advertising: Using Google Ads, Facebook Ads, and other platforms for targeted reach.

2. EFFECTIVE DIGITAL Marketing Strategies

Step 1: Define Your Target Audience

Understand demographics, preferences, and online behavior.

Use analytics tools to refine your audience segmentation.

STEP 2: CREATE HIGH-Quality Content

Develop blog posts, videos, and infographics that provide value.

Use storytelling and authentic branding to connect with customers.

STEP 3: OPTIMIZE FOR SEO and Social Media

Implement keyword research to improve search rankings.

Engage with followers through interactive posts and live sessions.

STEP 4: LEVERAGE PAID Advertising

Test different ad formats to see what works best.

Optimize campaigns for higher return on investment (ROI).

3. CHALLENGES IN DIGITAL Marketing

Constant Algorithm Changes: Stay updated with platform updates.

Market Saturation: Stand out by offering unique value propositions.

Budget Constraints: Allocate resources effectively for maximum impact.

FINAL ADVICE FOR DIGITAL Marketing Success

Focus on providing value and authenticity to your audience.

Analyze data to improve marketing strategies continuously.

Stay adaptable and explore new trends like AI-driven marketing.

DIGITAL MARKETING IS a powerful tool that, when mastered, can significantly boost profits. Implement these strategies to achieve long-term success in the online space!

Chapter 23: Financial Management for Sustainable Business Growth and Alternative Income Streams

Why Financial Management Matters

Proper financial management ensures business sustainability, while exploring alternative income streams provides financial security and wealth diversification. A well-balanced approach allows individuals and businesses to grow steadily.

1. MANAGING BUSINESS Finances Effectively

a. Budgeting and Expense Tracking

Create a detailed budget to manage business and personal finances.

Use financial tracking tools to monitor income and expenditures.

B. CASH FLOW MANAGEMENT

Maintain a positive cash flow to cover operational costs and future investments.

Implement strategies to reduce unnecessary expenses.

C. INVESTING IN GROWTH

Reinvest profits into business expansion and marketing efforts.

Consider hiring financial advisors for wealth management.

2. EXPLORING ALTERNATIVE Income Streams

a. Freelancing and Consulting

Leverage professional skills to offer services online.

Platforms like Upwork, Fiverr, and Freelancer provide remote work opportunities.

B. STOCK MARKET AND Cryptocurrency Investments

Learn stock trading basics and invest wisely.

Explore cryptocurrency and blockchain opportunities cautiously.

C. PASSIVE INCOME SOURCES

Earn through dividends, royalties, or rental properties.

Create digital products like e-books, courses, and print-on-demand merchandise.

D. AFFILIATE MARKETING and Online Monetization

Promote products and earn commissions through affiliate programs.

Monetize social media, YouTube, or blogs via advertising and sponsorships.

3. MANAGING DEBT AND Credit Wisely

Avoid excessive debt and prioritize high-interest payments.

Build and maintain a strong credit score for better financial opportunities.

4. SAVING AND EMERGENCY Funds

Set aside emergency savings for unforeseen circumstances.

Implement automated savings plans for financial security.

5. MEASURING FINANCIAL Success and Planning for the Future

Track income growth and evaluate investment returns.

Plan for retirement with diversified savings and investment strategies.

FINAL THOUGHTS

Sustainable financial management and multiple income streams provide financial freedom. By balancing business growth, alternative income sources, and smart investment strategies, individuals can achieve financial stability and long-term success.

In the next chapter, we will explore practical strategies for leveraging real estate investments and rental income opportunities.

CHAPTER 24: REAL ESTATE Investments and Rental Income Strategies

Why Real Estate is a Lucrative Investment

Real estate investments offer long-term financial stability, passive income, and wealth-building opportunities. Understanding the market and different investment strategies can maximize returns while minimizing risks.

1. TYPES OF REAL Estate Investments

a. Rental Properties

- Buy residential or commercial properties to generate monthly income.
- Screen tenants carefully to ensure timely rent payments.

b. House Flipping

- Purchase undervalued properties, renovate them, and sell at a profit.
- Requires market knowledge, renovation skills, and financial planning.

c. Real Estate Investment Trusts (REITs)

- Invest in real estate without owning property directly.
- Offers passive income through dividends.

d. Vacation Rentals (Airbnb & Short-Term Rentals)

- Rent out properties on a short-term basis to travelers.
- High profitability in popular tourist destinations.

e. Land Investment

- Buy undeveloped land and hold for future appreciation or development.
- Can be used for farming, leasing, or resale.

2. STEPS TO SUCCESSFUL Real Estate Investment

Step 1: Research the Market

- Analyze real estate trends and property values.
- Consider location, demand, and economic conditions.

Step 2: Secure Financing

- Explore mortgage options, real estate loans, or private funding.
- Maintain good credit for favorable loan terms.

Step 3: Choose the Right Property

- Look for properties with high appreciation potential and rental demand.

- Evaluate property condition, neighborhood, and amenities.

Step 4: Manage Properties Efficiently

- Hire property managers or use online tools for maintenance and rent collection.
- Ensure legal compliance with tenant agreements and property regulations.

3. GENERATING PASSIVE Income from Real Estate

- Use rental income to cover mortgage payments and expenses.
- Reinvest profits into additional properties to grow wealth.
- Consider real estate crowdfunding for low-cost investment entry.

4. RISKS AND HOW to Mitigate Them

- **Market Fluctuations**: Stay updated on economic trends and diversify investments.
- **Vacancies**: Set competitive rent prices and offer incentives to attract tenants.
- **Maintenance Costs**: Budget for repairs and unexpected expenses.

5. MEASURING REAL Estate Investment Success

- Track return on investment (ROI) and cash flow.
- Compare rental income to expenses to ensure profitability.
- Adjust strategies based on market conditions and financial goals.

FINAL THOUGHTS

Real estate can be a powerful tool for financial growth when managed wisely. By investing strategically, mitigating risks, and maximizing rental income, investors can create long-term wealth.

In the next chapter, we will explore the world of e-commerce and how to build a profitable online store.

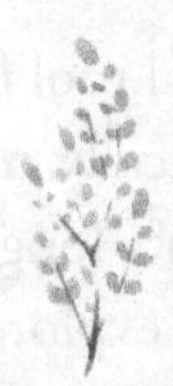

Chapter 25: Building a Profitable E-Commerce Business

Why E-Commerce is a Lucrative Opportunity

E-commerce offers a flexible and scalable business model with a global reach. With low startup costs and various platforms available, anyone can build an online store and generate significant revenue.

1. CHOOSING THE RIGHT E-Commerce Model

a. Dropshipping

Sell products without holding inventory.

Suppliers handle storage and shipping.

B. PRINT-ON-DEMAND

Sell custom-designed products (t-shirts, mugs, posters, etc.).

Products are created and shipped only when orders are placed.

C. PRIVATE LABELING & Manufacturing

Create a unique brand by sourcing or manufacturing products.

Requires inventory management and quality control.

D. DIGITAL PRODUCTS & Services

Sell e-books, courses, software, or memberships.

High-profit margins with no physical inventory needed.

E. SUBSCRIPTION-BASED Business

Offer recurring services or products on a subscription model.

Examples: Monthly snack boxes, fitness programs, or software services.

2. SETTING UP YOUR Online Store

Step 1: Choose a Platform

Shopify, WooCommerce, BigCommerce, or Wix for website-based stores.

Amazon, eBay, or Etsy for marketplace-based selling.

STEP 2: PICK A NICHE and Products

Identify in-demand, profitable products with low competition.

Conduct market research to validate ideas.

STEP 3: BUILD YOUR Brand

Create a unique logo, website design, and brand identity.

Develop a compelling brand story to connect with customers.

STEP 4: SET UP PAYMENT & Shipping

Integrate payment gateways (PayPal, Stripe, etc.).

Offer competitive shipping options and free shipping incentives.

3. DRIVING TRAFFIC to Your E-Commerce Store

Search Engine Optimization (SEO): Optimize product listings for Google rankings.

Social Media Marketing: Promote products on Instagram, Facebook, TikTok, and Pinterest.

Influencer Collaborations: Partner with social media influencers to boost credibility.

Email Marketing: Build an email list and nurture potential customers with promotions.

Paid Advertising: Utilize Google Ads, Facebook Ads, and TikTok Ads to drive targeted traffic.

4. SCALING AND AUTOMATING Your Business

Use chatbots and AI tools for customer support.

Implement email automation to increase sales conversions.

Expand to global markets by offering worldwide shipping.

Outsource tasks like fulfillment and customer service to focus on growth.

5. MEASURING SUCCESS and Adapting Strategies

Track key metrics like conversion rates, average order value, and customer retention.

Continuously optimize product offerings based on market demand.

Stay updated with e-commerce trends and evolving customer preferences.

FINAL THOUGHTS

Building a profitable e-commerce business requires dedication, creativity, and strategic marketing. By choosing the right model, optimizing operations, and leveraging digital marketing, entrepreneurs can create a sustainable online income stream.

In the next chapter, we will explore content creation and how to make money through blogging, YouTube, and social media.

Chapter 26: Monetizing Content Creation – Blogging, YouTube & Social Media

Why Content Creation is a Lucrative Opportunity

Content creation allows individuals to earn money by sharing valuable, entertaining, or educational content online. With multiple monetization methods, bloggers, YouTubers, and social media influencers can turn their passion into a profitable business.

1. CHOOSING YOUR CONTENT Niche

Personal Finance & Investing: Teach financial literacy and investment strategies.

Health & Fitness: Share workout routines, diet tips, and wellness advice.

Technology & Gaming: Review gadgets, software, and video games.

DIY & Crafts: Provide step-by-step tutorials for homemade projects.

Entertainment & Lifestyle: Create vlogs, reaction videos, or travel content.

Education & Self-Improvement: Teach skills like coding, languages, or business strategies.

2. MONETIZING A BLOG

Step 1: Start a Blog

Choose a niche and domain name.

Use platforms like WordPress or Medium.

Optimize for SEO to drive organic traffic.

STEP 2: MONETIZATION Strategies

Google AdSense & Display Ads: Earn revenue from site traffic.

Affiliate Marketing: Promote products and earn commissions.

Sponsored Posts: Collaborate with brands to create paid content.

Selling Digital Products: Offer e-books, courses, or templates.

3. MAKING MONEY ON YouTube

Step 1: Set Up a YouTube Channel

Choose a niche and create high-quality videos.

Optimize video titles, descriptions, and tags for search.

STEP 2: MONETIZATION Strategies

YouTube Partner Program: Earn ad revenue from views.

Sponsorships & Brand Deals: Partner with companies for paid promotions.

Merchandise Sales: Sell branded products through YouTube's Merch Shelf.

Channel Memberships & Super Chats: Offer exclusive content for paying subscribers.

4. EARNING FROM SOCIAL Media

Step 1: Build a Social Media Presence

Choose platforms like Instagram, TikTok, Twitter, or Facebook.

Engage with followers and post consistently.

STEP 2: MONETIZATION Strategies

Sponsored Content: Partner with brands for paid posts.

Affiliate Marketing: Share referral links to earn commissions.

Exclusive Content Subscriptions: Use platforms like Patreon or OnlyFans.

Selling Products & Services: Offer physical or digital goods.

5. GROWING YOUR AUDIENCE and Maximizing Earnings

Consistency is Key: Post regularly to stay relevant.

Engage with Your Audience: Respond to comments and build a community.

Collaborate with Others: Partner with influencers to reach new audiences.

Analyze Performance: Use analytics tools to track growth and adjust strategies.

FINAL THOUGHTS

Content creation can be a full-time career with limitless potential. By leveraging multiple monetization methods and continuously improving content quality, creators can establish a stable and lucrative income stream.

In the next chapter, we will explore freelance work and gig economy jobs as another way to earn money online.

Chapter 27: Freelancing & Gig Economy Jobs – Turning Skills into Income

Why Freelancing is a Great Way to Earn Money

Freelancing allows individuals to work independently, offering their skills and expertise to clients worldwide. The gig economy provides numerous opportunities to earn money without a traditional job structure.

1. IDENTIFYING YOUR Marketable Skills

Writing & Editing: Content writing, copywriting, proofreading.

Graphic Design & Video Editing: Logos, social media posts, animations.

Programming & Web Development: Website creation, app development, software engineering.

Digital Marketing & SEO: Social media management, advertising, email marketing.

Virtual Assistance & Customer Support: Admin tasks, scheduling, customer service.

Tutoring & Coaching: Online teaching, mentorship, language instruction.

2. FINDING FREELANCE Work

Step 1: Choose a Freelance Platform

Upwork & Fiverr: Popular marketplaces for freelancers.

Freelancer & PeoplePerHour: Alternative platforms with various job postings.

Toptal & 99Designs: Premium platforms for high-level professionals.

STEP 2: BUILD A STRONG Profile

Showcase previous work and testimonials.

Set competitive rates and clear service descriptions.

STEP 3: APPLY FOR JOBS & Build a Portfolio

Start with small projects to gain experience.

Collect positive reviews to attract more clients.

3. GIG ECONOMY JOBS for Quick Income

Ridesharing (Uber, Lyft): Earn by driving passengers.

Food & Grocery Delivery (DoorDash, UberEats): Deliver meals and groceries.

Task-Based Jobs (TaskRabbit, Gigwalk): Perform errands and small tasks.

Pet Sitting & House Sitting (Rover, TrustedHousesitters): Get paid to care for pets or houses.

Online Surveys & Testing (UserTesting, Swagbucks): Earn money by testing apps and websites.

4. MAXIMIZING FREELANCE Earnings

Specialize in High-Demand Skills: Increase your value in the market.

Network & Market Yourself: Use LinkedIn and social media to find clients.

Improve Time Management: Balance multiple projects effectively.

Raise Your Rates Over Time: As experience grows, charge higher fees.

5. FREELANCING AS A Long-Term Career

Build a Personal Brand: Develop a website and showcase expertise.

Expand to Passive Income Streams: Create courses, write e-books, or start consulting.

Transition to an Agency Model: Hire other freelancers and scale your business.

FINAL THOUGHTS

Freelancing and gig work provide financial independence and flexibility. By identifying your skills, finding clients, and consistently improving your services, you can create a sustainable income stream.

In the next chapter, we will explore real estate investing and how it can generate long-term wealth.

Chapter 28: Real Estate Investing – Building Wealth Through Property

Why Real Estate is a Powerful Investment

Real estate is one of the most reliable ways to build long-term wealth. Property investments offer passive income, appreciation, and financial security when managed wisely.

1. UNDERSTANDING REAL Estate Investment Types

Residential Properties: Rental homes, apartments, vacation rentals.

Commercial Properties: Office spaces, retail stores, warehouses.

Industrial Properties: Factories, storage facilities, logistics centers.

Real Estate Investment Trusts (REITs): Stocks in real estate companies for passive investment.

Fix-and-Flip: Buying undervalued homes, renovating, and reselling for profit.

2. GETTING STARTED in Real Estate Investing

Step 1: Determine Your Investment Budget

Assess financial health and credit score.

Save for a down payment and closing costs.

Consider mortgage options and loan pre-approval.

STEP 2: CHOOSE AN INVESTMENT Strategy

Buy and Hold: Purchase property and rent it for passive income.

Flipping: Invest in undervalued properties, renovate, and sell.

Short-Term Rentals: Utilize platforms like Airbnb for higher rental income.

Real Estate Crowdfunding: Join group investments in large projects.

STEP 3: RESEARCH THE Market

Analyze local real estate trends and property appreciation.

Identify high-demand areas with growth potential.

Compare rental yields and property values.

3. MANAGING YOUR REAL Estate Investment

Finding Tenants: Screen applicants and establish rental agreements.

Property Maintenance: Regular upkeep to retain value and attract renters.

Hiring a Property Manager: Manage rentals efficiently without direct involvement.

Tax Benefits & Deductions: Leverage tax advantages for property owners.

4. SCALING YOUR REAL Estate Portfolio

Reinvest Profits: Use rental income to acquire additional properties.

Leverage Home Equity: Refinance properties to fund new investments.

Diversify Investments: Explore different types of real estate to balance risks.

5. AVOIDING COMMON Real Estate Pitfalls

Overleveraging: Avoid excessive debt that leads to financial strain.

Neglecting Market Research: Always analyze the location before buying.

Underestimating Costs: Budget for maintenance, taxes, and unexpected expenses.

Ignoring Legal Requirements: Understand zoning laws, rental regulations, and property rights.

FINAL THOUGHTS

Real estate investing is a proven wealth-building strategy. With proper planning, research, and management, it can generate passive income and long-term financial security.

In the next chapter, we will explore the stock market and how to invest in stocks for steady returns.

Chapter 29: Stock Market Investing – Growing Wealth Through Stocks

Why Invest in the Stock Market?

The stock market is a powerful vehicle for wealth accumulation. By investing in stocks, individuals can benefit from long-term growth, dividends, and portfolio diversification.

1. UNDERSTANDING STOCKS and How They Work

Common Stocks: Provide ownership in a company and potential dividends.

Preferred Stocks: Offer fixed dividends and priority in company earnings.

ETFs (Exchange-Traded Funds): A diversified mix of stocks for risk reduction.

Mutual Funds: Professionally managed funds investing in multiple stocks.

Index Funds: Passive investments that track major stock indices (e.g., S&P 500).

2. STEPS TO START INVESTING in Stocks

Step 1: Open a Brokerage Account

Choose a brokerage platform with low fees and a user-friendly interface.

Consider options like Robinhood, E-Trade, Fidelity, or TD Ameritrade.

STEP 2: DETERMINE YOUR Investment Strategy

Growth Investing: Focus on high-potential companies with rapid expansion.

Value Investing: Buy undervalued stocks with strong fundamentals.

Dividend Investing: Invest in stocks that provide consistent dividends.

Index Investing: Passively invest in broad market indices for long-term stability.

STEP 3: RESEARCH AND Select Stocks

Analyze financial statements and earnings reports.

Evaluate industry trends and company performance.

Diversify holdings to mitigate risk.

3. MANAGING AND GROWING Your Stock Portfolio

Monitor Investments: Regularly track market trends and company news.

Reinvest Dividends: Use earnings to purchase additional shares.

Adjust Portfolio as Needed: Rebalance based on performance and goals.

Utilize Dollar-Cost Averaging: Invest fixed amounts regularly to reduce volatility.

4. RISKS AND HOW TO Mitigate Them

Market Volatility: Accept fluctuations and focus on long-term growth.

Economic Downturns: Diversify investments to reduce exposure.

Company-Specific Risks: Research thoroughly before investing.

Emotional Investing: Avoid panic selling during market downturns.

5. BUILDING LONG-TERM Wealth Through Stocks

Start Early and Stay Consistent: The power of compounding benefits long-term investors.

Diversify Your Portfolio: Reduce risks by investing across industries.

Have a Clear Exit Strategy: Know when to take profits or cut losses.

Stay Informed: Follow market news and continually learn about investing.

FINAL THOUGHTS

Stock market investing provides opportunities for financial growth and wealth creation. With patience, research, and discipline, individuals can achieve financial independence through stock investments.

In the next chapter, we will explore cryptocurrency investments and how digital assets can be leveraged for financial gains.

Chapter 30: Cryptocurrency Investing – Navigating the Digital Asset Market

Why Invest in Cryptocurrency?

Cryptocurrency has emerged as a new financial frontier, offering opportunities for high returns, decentralized finance, and technological innovation. Digital assets like Bitcoin and Ethereum have gained mainstream acceptance, making them viable investment options.

1. UNDERSTANDING CRYPTOCURRENCIES

Bitcoin (BTC): The first and most widely recognized cryptocurrency.

Ethereum (ETH): A blockchain platform enabling smart contracts and decentralized applications.

Altcoins: Alternative cryptocurrencies like Solana (SOL), Binance Coin (BNB), and Cardano (ADA).

Stablecoins: Cryptocurrencies pegged to stable assets like the US dollar (e.g., USDT, USDC).

NFTs (Non-Fungible Tokens): Unique digital assets representing ownership of art, music, and more.

2. STEPS TO START INVESTING in Cryptocurrency

Step 1: Choose a Cryptocurrency Exchange

Select a reliable exchange such as Binance, Coinbase, Kraken, or KuCoin.

Ensure the platform offers security features like two-factor authentication (2FA).

STEP 2: SECURE YOUR Investments

Use hardware wallets (Ledger, Trezor) for long-term storage.

Enable strong passwords and backup recovery phrases.

STEP 3: BUILD A DIVERSIFIED Crypto Portfolio

Invest in multiple cryptocurrencies to mitigate risk.

Allocate funds based on risk tolerance and investment goals.

3. STRATEGIES FOR CRYPTOCURRENCY Investing

HODLing: Buy and hold for long-term gains.

Day Trading: Profit from short-term price fluctuations.

Staking: Earn passive income by holding and validating transactions.

Yield Farming: Lend crypto assets to earn rewards.

4. RISKS AND HOW TO Manage Them

Market Volatility: Cryptocurrency prices can fluctuate significantly.

Security Risks: Protect assets from hacks, scams, and phishing attacks.

Regulatory Uncertainty: Governments may impose regulations affecting the market.

Liquidity Issues: Some cryptocurrencies have low trading volumes, making them harder to sell.

5. LONG-TERM CRYPTOCURRENCY Investment Strategies

Research Before Investing: Understand the technology and use cases behind each cryptocurrency.

Stay Updated: Follow news, trends, and regulatory developments.

Use Dollar-Cost Averaging (DCA): Invest consistently over time to reduce risk.

Avoid FOMO (Fear of Missing Out): Stick to an investment plan and avoid impulsive decisions.

FINAL THOUGHTS

Cryptocurrency investing offers exciting opportunities but requires caution, education, and security measures. By understanding the market and employing the right strategies, investors can benefit from this evolving financial landscape.

In the next chapter, we will explore passive income streams and how to generate consistent earnings without active involvement.

Chapter 31: Passive Income – Earning Money with Minimal Effort

Why Pursue Passive Income?

Passive income allows individuals to earn money continuously with little to no daily involvement. It provides financial freedom, stability, and the potential to build wealth over time.

1. UNDERSTANDING PASSIVE Income

Active vs. Passive Income: Active income requires direct work (e.g., salary), while passive income generates earnings with minimal effort (e.g., rental income, investments).

Benefits of Passive Income: Financial independence, wealth accumulation, and flexibility in work-life balance.

2. TYPES OF PASSIVE Income Streams

Investing-Based Income

Dividend Stocks: Earn regular payouts from company profits.

Bonds & Fixed Deposits: Receive interest payments over time.

Real Estate Rentals: Generate income by leasing property.

ONLINE BUSINESS & DIGITAL Products

Affiliate Marketing: Promote products and earn commissions.

E-Books & Online Courses: Sell digital knowledge-based products.

YouTube & Blogging: Monetize content through ads and sponsorships.

AUTOMATION & ROYALTIES

App Development: Earn from in-app purchases and subscriptions.

Music & Book Royalties: Receive payments from intellectual property rights.

Dropshipping & Print-on-Demand: Sell products online without handling inventory.

3. STEPS TO CREATE Passive Income Streams

Step 1: Identify Your Strengths & Interests

Choose passive income methods aligned with your skills and passion.

STEP 2: RESEARCH & Start Small

Analyze market trends and test strategies with minimal investment.

STEP 3: AUTOMATE & Scale

Use technology and outsourcing to increase earnings while reducing effort.

4. OVERCOMING CHALLENGES in Passive Income Generation

Initial Time & Effort: Some passive income streams require upfront work.

Market Fluctuations: Investments and online income can be unpredictable.

Scalability & Competition: Success depends on differentiation and continuous optimization.

5. LONG-TERM STRATEGIES for Sustainable Passive Income

Diversify Income Sources: Avoid reliance on a single stream of revenue.

Reinvest Earnings: Use profits to expand and create additional income channels.

Stay Updated: Monitor industry trends and adapt to new opportunities.

Maintain Financial Discipline: Save and invest wisely to secure long-term benefits.

FINAL THOUGHTS

Passive income is an excellent way to achieve financial stability and freedom. By leveraging investments, online platforms, and automation, individuals can create sustainable revenue with minimal daily effort.

In the next chapter, we will explore franchising and how it can serve as a profitable business model for aspiring entrepreneurs.

Chapter 32: Franchising – Building a Business with Proven Success

Why Consider Franchising?

Franchising offers an opportunity to run a business using an established brand, proven operational model, and built-in customer base. It reduces the risks associated with starting a business from scratch while providing training and support.

1. UNDERSTANDING FRANCHISING

What is a Franchise? A business arrangement where an individual (franchisee) buys the rights to operate under an established brand (franchisor).

Types of Franchises:

Product Distribution Franchise (e.g., automobile dealerships, soft drink distributors).

Business Format Franchise (e.g., fast-food chains, retail stores).

Manufacturing Franchise (e.g., beverage companies granting bottling rights).

BENEFITS OF FRANCHISING:

Recognized brand and customer loyalty.

Access to a proven business model and training.

Support from the franchisor in marketing and operations.

Easier access to financing.

2. STEPS TO OWNING a Franchise

Step 1: Research Franchise Opportunities

Analyze different industries and brands.

Consider startup costs, profitability, and support provided by the franchisor.

Evaluate franchise success rates and market demand.

STEP 2: FINANCIAL PREPARATION

Understand franchise fees, royalties, and initial investment requirements.

Secure funding through savings, loans, or investors.

Prepare a business plan to present to lenders or investors.

STEP 3: LEGAL CONSIDERATIONS

Review the Franchise Disclosure Document (FDD) carefully.

Consult a franchise attorney to understand rights and obligations.

Ensure compliance with local business laws and regulations.

STEP 4: LOCATION & Setup

Choose an ideal location based on customer traffic and demographics.

Work with the franchisor to design and equip the franchise.

Hire and train employees according to franchise standards.

STEP 5: MARKETING & Growth

Utilize franchisor-provided marketing materials and strategies.

Engage with the local community to increase visibility.

Monitor performance and follow the franchisor's operational guidelines.

3. CHALLENGES OF FRANCHISING and How to Overcome Them

High Initial Investment: Consider financing options or start with a lower-cost franchise.

Limited Operational Control: Adhere to franchisor guidelines but find ways to personalize customer service.

Market Saturation: Research competition in your chosen location before investing.

Royalties and Fees: Factor ongoing costs into financial planning to maintain profitability.

4. LONG-TERM STRATEGIES for Franchise Success

Commit to Continuous Learning: Attend franchisor training and industry events.

Focus on Customer Experience: Maintain high-quality service to build loyalty.

Expand Wisely: Consider opening additional locations once the first is successful.

Build a Strong Relationship with the Franchisor: Regularly communicate and seek guidance.

FINAL THOUGHTS

Franchising provides a structured path to entrepreneurship with reduced risk. By leveraging an established brand and support system, franchise owners can achieve long-term success with dedication and strategic planning.

In the next chapter, we will explore stock market investing and how to build wealth through smart equity investments.

Chapter 33: Stock Market Investing – Growing Wealth Through Equities

Why Invest in the Stock Market?

The stock market provides an opportunity to grow wealth over time by investing in companies that generate profits. While it involves risk, strategic investing can lead to significant financial gains.

1. UNDERSTANDING STOCK Market Basics

What is the Stock Market? A platform where investors buy and sell shares of publicly traded companies.

Types of Stocks:

Common Stocks: Ownership in a company with voting rights and potential dividends.

Preferred Stocks: Higher claim on earnings and dividends but usually no voting rights.

STOCK EXCHANGES: MAJOR platforms like the New York Stock Exchange (NYSE) and NASDAQ facilitate stock trading.

Stock Market Indices: Benchmarks like the S&P 500 and Dow Jones Industrial Average track market performance.

2. HOW TO START INVESTING in Stocks

Step 1: Educate Yourself

Learn key financial terms (e.g., market capitalization, earnings per share, price-to-earnings ratio).

Follow financial news and study market trends.

STEP 2: SET INVESTMENT Goals

Determine short-term and long-term financial objectives.

Choose between growth investing (high-risk, high-reward) and dividend investing (steady income).

STEP 3: OPEN A BROKERAGE Account

Compare brokerage platforms based on fees, research tools, and ease of use.

Consider robo-advisors for automated portfolio management.

STEP 4: RESEARCH AND Select Stocks

Analyze company fundamentals (e.g., revenue, profit margins, debt levels).

Study historical price trends and stock performance.

STEP 5: BUILD A DIVERSIFIED Portfolio

Invest in various sectors to mitigate risks.

Allocate funds between individual stocks, ETFs, and mutual funds.

STEP 6: MONITOR AND Adjust Investments

Regularly review stock performance and economic conditions.
Rebalance portfolio to align with financial goals.

3. RISKS AND CHALLENGES of Stock Market Investing

Market Volatility: Stock prices fluctuate due to economic events and investor sentiment.

Company-Specific Risks: Poor management or financial struggles can impact stock value.

Emotional Investing: Avoid panic selling and impulsive decisions.

Lack of Diversification: Overinvesting in one stock increases financial risk.

4. LONG-TERM STRATEGIES for Stock Market Success

Invest for the Long Run: Hold stocks for years to benefit from compound growth.

Reinvest Dividends: Use dividend payouts to buy more shares and accelerate wealth accumulation.

Stay Informed: Keep up with market news and adjust strategies accordingly.

Adopt a Disciplined Approach: Stick to a well-planned investment strategy and avoid emotional reactions.

FINAL THOUGHTS

Stock market investing is a powerful tool for wealth-building. By understanding market fundamentals, managing risks, and adopting a long-term perspective, investors can achieve financial growth.

In the next chapter, we will explore cryptocurrency investments and how to navigate the digital asset market.

Chapter 34: Cryptocurrency Investing – Navigating the Digital Asset Market

Why Invest in Cryptocurrency?

Cryptocurrency is a decentralized digital asset that offers financial opportunities outside traditional markets. With its potential for high returns and innovative blockchain technology, it has attracted global investors.

1. UNDERSTANDING CRYPTOCURRENCY Basics

What is Cryptocurrency? Digital currency secured by cryptography, enabling secure transactions.

Blockchain Technology: A decentralized ledger that records all crypto transactions.

Popular Cryptocurrencies:

Bitcoin (BTC): The first and most widely recognized cryptocurrency.

Ethereum (ETH): Known for smart contract capabilities.

Altcoins: Other digital currencies such as Binance Coin (BNB), Solana (SOL), and Cardano (ADA).

CRYPTO EXCHANGES: PLATFORMS like Binance, Coinbase, and Kraken allow users to buy, sell, and trade crypto assets.

2. HOW TO START INVESTING in Cryptocurrency

Step 1: Educate Yourself

Learn key terms like private keys, wallets, and decentralized finance (DeFi).

Understand the risks and regulatory environment.

STEP 2: CHOOSE A SECURE Exchange

Compare fees, security features, and available cryptocurrencies.

Use two-factor authentication (2FA) for added security.

STEP 3: SET UP A CRYPTO Wallet

Hot Wallets: Online wallets for easy access but with higher risks.

Cold Wallets: Offline wallets providing maximum security against hacks.

STEP 4: DEVELOP AN Investment Strategy

Decide between short-term trading and long-term holding (HODLing).

Diversify investments to manage risk.

STEP 5: MONITOR MARKET Trends

Keep track of price movements and news affecting the crypto market.

Utilize technical and fundamental analysis.

3. RISKS AND CHALLENGES of Cryptocurrency Investing

Market Volatility: Prices can fluctuate dramatically within hours.

Regulatory Uncertainty: Governments may impose restrictions or bans.

Security Threats: Crypto wallets and exchanges are frequent targets for hackers.

Lack of Consumer Protection: Transactions are irreversible, and fraud is prevalent.

4. LONG-TERM STRATEGIES for Cryptocurrency Success

Only Invest What You Can Afford to Lose: Crypto is highly speculative.

Stay Updated: Follow industry news, government regulations, and market developments.

Use Secure Storage: Store large investments in cold wallets for protection.

Take Advantage of Staking & Yield Farming: Earn passive income from holdings.

FINAL THOUGHTS

Cryptocurrency investing offers exciting opportunities but comes with significant risks. By educating yourself, securing assets properly, and employing strategic investing techniques, you can navigate the digital asset market successfully.

In the next chapter, we will explore real estate investing and how to build wealth through property ownership.

Chapter 35: Real Estate Investing – Building Wealth Through Property Ownership

Why Invest in Real Estate?

Real estate is a tangible asset that can generate income, appreciate in value, and provide financial security. Unlike stocks and cryptocurrencies, property investments offer stability and long-term wealth-building potential.

1. UNDERSTANDING REAL Estate Basics

What is Real Estate Investing? The purchase, ownership, management, rental, or sale of property for profit.

Types of Real Estate Investments:

Residential Properties: Houses, apartments, and condos.

Commercial Properties: Office spaces, retail stores, and warehouses.

Industrial Properties: Factories, distribution centers, and storage facilities.

Real Estate Investment Trusts (REITs): Companies that own and manage income-generating properties.

2. HOW TO START INVESTING in Real Estate

Step 1: Research the Market

Analyze property values, rental demand, and economic trends.

Identify high-growth areas with potential appreciation.

STEP 2: SET INVESTMENT Goals

Decide between rental income, property flipping, or long-term appreciation.

Determine your risk tolerance and financial commitment.

STEP 3: SECURE FINANCING

Consider mortgage loans, real estate crowdfunding, or partnerships.

Evaluate interest rates and loan terms before making a purchase.

STEP 4: FIND THE RIGHT Property

Work with real estate agents or explore listings independently.

Conduct property inspections and assess potential maintenance costs.

STEP 5: MANAGE YOUR Investment

Hire property managers or oversee rentals personally.

Maintain properties to ensure long-term value.

3. RISKS AND CHALLENGES of Real Estate Investing

Market Fluctuations: Property values can decline due to economic downturns.

High Initial Costs: Requires significant upfront capital for purchasing and maintenance.

Tenant Issues: Vacancies, late payments, or property damage can impact profitability.

Illiquidity: Selling real estate takes time compared to stocks or cryptocurrencies.

4. LONG-TERM STRATEGIES for Real Estate Success

Buy and Hold: Acquire properties in growth areas and rent them for steady income.

Flipping Properties: Purchase undervalued homes, renovate, and sell for a profit.

Diversify Your Portfolio: Invest in different property types to minimize risks.

Leverage REITs: Gain real estate exposure without property ownership.

FINAL THOUGHTS

Real estate is a powerful wealth-building tool that provides both income and appreciation. By choosing the right properties, managing risks, and adopting a long-term perspective, investors can achieve financial success.

In the next chapter, we will explore passive income strategies and how to generate revenue without active involvement.

Chapter 36: Passive Income Strategies – Earning Money While You Sleep

Why Focus on Passive Income?

Passive income allows you to earn money without active daily involvement. It provides financial freedom, stability, and long-term wealth-building opportunities.

1. UNDERSTANDING PASSIVE Income

What is Passive Income? Revenue generated with minimal effort after the initial setup.

Benefits of Passive Income:

Reduces reliance on traditional employment.

Provides financial security and flexibility.

Enables wealth accumulation over time.

2. TOP PASSIVE INCOME Strategies

1. Dividend Stocks

Invest in dividend-paying companies for regular payouts.

Reinvest dividends for compound growth.

2. REAL ESTATE RENTALS

Purchase properties and rent them out for consistent income.

Use property managers to handle maintenance and tenants.

3. PEER-TO-PEER LENDING

Lend money through online platforms and earn interest.

Assess borrower risk to maximize returns.

4. AFFILIATE MARKETING

Promote products/services through blogs, websites, or social media.

Earn commissions on sales generated through your links.

5. CREATE DIGITAL PRODUCTS

Sell eBooks, courses, or printables online.

Utilize platforms like Amazon Kindle, Teachable, or Etsy.

6. MONETIZE A BLOG or YouTube Channel

Generate ad revenue through content creation.

Leverage sponsorships and brand deals.

7. AUTOMATED DROPSHIPPING Business

Sell products online without handling inventory.

Automate order fulfillment through suppliers.

8. INVEST IN REITS (Real Estate Investment Trusts)

Own shares in income-generating real estate without managing properties.

Earn dividends from real estate portfolios.

9. LICENSING AND ROYALTIES

License intellectual property, such as music, photos, or software.

Earn royalties from books, patents, or creative content.

10. HIGH-YIELD SAVINGS and Investments

Earn interest from savings accounts, bonds, and dividend funds.

Utilize robo-advisors for automated investment management.

3. STEPS TO BUILD A Passive Income Portfolio

Step 1: Assess Your Skills and Resources

Identify areas where you have expertise or capital to invest.

Research passive income methods that align with your interests.

STEP 2: START SMALL and Scale Up

Experiment with one or two strategies before expanding.

Reinvent and optimize income streams over time.

STEP 3: AUTOMATE AND Outsource

Use software, virtual assistants, or third-party services to reduce workload.

Focus on scalability to maximize earnings.

STEP 4: MONITOR AND Adjust

Track earnings and optimize strategies for better results.

Reinvest passive income for greater financial growth.

FINAL THOUGHTS

Building passive income takes time and effort upfront, but the long-term rewards are substantial. By diversifying income streams, automating processes, and staying consistent, you can achieve financial independence.

In the next chapter, we will explore freelancing and side hustles, showing how to turn skills into income.

Chapter 37: Freelancing and Side Hustles – Turning Skills into Income

Why Consider Freelancing and Side Hustles?

Freelancing and side hustles provide flexible opportunities to earn money using your skills. They can supplement your primary income or evolve into full-time businesses.

1. UNDERSTANDING FREELANCING and Side Hustles

Freelancing: Offering services on a project or contract basis without committing to a single employer.

Side Hustles: Small businesses or part-time jobs pursued alongside a main source of income.

Benefits:

Work on your own schedule.

Earn additional income.

Gain experience and build a portfolio.

Potential for business growth.

2. POPULAR FREELANCING and Side Hustle Opportunities

1. Writing and Content Creation

Blog writing, copywriting, technical writing, and ghostwriting.

Platforms: Upwork, Fiverr, Freelancer, and Medium.

2. GRAPHIC DESIGN AND Illustration

Logo creation, branding, web design, and social media graphics.

Tools: Adobe Illustrator, Canva, and Figma.

3. VIDEO EDITING AND Animation

Editing YouTube videos, creating motion graphics, and producing explainer videos.

Platforms: Adobe Premiere Pro, Final Cut Pro, and After Effects.

4. PROGRAMMING AND Web Development

Building websites, mobile apps, and software solutions.

Platforms: GitHub, Upwork, and Toptal.

5. SOCIAL MEDIA MANAGEMENT

Managing accounts, content scheduling, and digital marketing.

Platforms: Hootsuite, Buffer, and Meta Business Suite.

6. SELLING DIGITAL Products

eBooks, courses, stock photos, and printables.

Platforms: Gumroad, Etsy, and Teachable.

7. ONLINE TUTORING and Coaching

Teaching academic subjects, language learning, or personal development skills.

Platforms: VIPKid, Teachable, and Udemy.

8. DROPSHIPPING AND E-commerce

Selling products without managing inventory.

Platforms: Shopify, WooCommerce, and AliExpress.

9. VIRTUAL ASSISTANCE

Administrative support, email management, and appointment scheduling.

Platforms: Zirtual, Belay, and Time Etc.

10. PRINT-ON-DEMAND Business

Designing and selling custom apparel, accessories, and home decor.

Platforms: Printful, Redbubble, and Teespring.

3. STEPS TO START A Successful Freelance or Side Hustle Career

Step 1: Identify Your Skills and Interests

Choose something you're good at and passionate about.

Research demand and potential earnings.

STEP 2: BUILD A PORTFOLIO and Online Presence

Showcase previous work through a personal website or portfolio.

Create LinkedIn, social media, or freelancer profiles.

STEP 3: FIND CLIENTS and Opportunities

Use freelance platforms and networking to secure projects.

Offer competitive rates and outstanding service to build a reputation.

STEP 4: MANAGE YOUR Work and Scale Up

Set schedules, deadlines, and pricing.

Automate processes and outsource tasks as your business grows.

FINAL THOUGHTS

Freelancing and side hustles can provide significant income and career opportunities. By leveraging your skills, marketing your services, and staying consistent, you can turn a small gig into a profitable venture.

In the next chapter, we will explore investing in stocks and cryptocurrencies to grow your wealth further.

Chapter 38: Creating a Legacy Through Smart Financial Decisions

Why Build a Financial Legacy?

Leaving a financial legacy means ensuring long-term stability for yourself and future generations. It's about making intelligent financial decisions that create lasting wealth beyond your lifetime.

1. THE COMPONENTS OF a Strong Financial Legacy

Wealth Accumulation: Earning and growing money through smart investments.

Asset Protection: Safeguarding wealth from inflation, taxes, and legal risks.

Generational Wealth Transfer: Passing on financial security to your heirs.

Philanthropy and Giving Back: Creating a positive impact on society.

2. STRATEGIES FOR BUILDING Long-Term Wealth

Step 1: Invest for the Future

Maximize compound interest through long-term investments.

Focus on stocks, bonds, real estate, and businesses.

STEP 2: PROTECT YOUR Wealth

Utilize trusts, insurance, and legal structures to secure assets.

Diversify investments to reduce risk and preserve value.

STEP 3: EDUCATE THE Next Generation

Teach financial literacy to family members.

Encourage smart financial habits early on.

STEP 4: GIVE BACK STRATEGICALLY

Set up charitable foundations or scholarships.

Use tax-efficient giving strategies to maximize impact.

3. CHALLENGES IN LEGACY Planning

Market Volatility: Build a resilient portfolio to withstand downturns.

Tax Liabilities: Use legal strategies to minimize estate taxes.

Family Disputes: Establish clear inheritance plans and wills.

FINAL ADVICE FOR BUILDING a Lasting Financial Legacy

Start now—the earlier you plan, the stronger your legacy.

Balance wealth creation and life enjoyment.

Regularly update your financial plans to adapt to economic changes.

A FINANCIAL LEGACY is not just about wealth—it's about creating security, opportunity, and impact for future generations. Take the right steps today to ensure a prosperous tomorrow!

Chapter 39: Real Estate Investment – Building Wealth Through Property

Why Invest in Real Estate?

Real estate offers a tangible and stable way to grow wealth. Unlike stocks or cryptocurrencies, properties provide long-term appreciation, rental income, and tax benefits.

1. UNDERSTANDING REAL Estate Investment

Types of Real Estate Investments

Residential Properties: Homes, apartments, and rental units.

Commercial Properties: Office buildings, retail spaces, and warehouses.

Real Estate Investment Trusts (REITs): Investment in real estate through publicly traded companies.

2. BENEFITS OF REAL Estate Investment

Stable Income from Rentals

Property Value Appreciation

Tax Advantages (Depreciation, Deductions)

Leverage to Acquire More Assets

3. HOW TO START INVESTING in Real Estate

Step 1: Research the Market

Understand location trends, property values, and rental demand.

STEP 2: SECURE FINANCING

Explore mortgage options, loans, and down payment strategies.

STEP 3: CHOOSE THE Right Property

Assess potential rental income and long-term appreciation.

STEP 4: MANAGE AND Maintain the Property

Consider hiring a property manager or handling tenants yourself.

4. RISKS AND CHALLENGES

Market Fluctuations: Property values can rise and fall.

High Initial Capital: Real estate requires significant investment.

Maintenance and Repairs: Ongoing costs can be substantial.

FINAL ADVICE FOR REAL Estate Investment

Start small with rental properties before expanding.

Always conduct thorough due diligence before purchasing.

Diversify within real estate (residential, commercial, REITs) to minimize risk.

Chapter 40: The Road to Financial Independence – Achieving Long-Term Wealth

What is Financial Independence?

Financial independence means having enough assets or passive income to cover your living expenses without needing a traditional job. It allows freedom to pursue passions, travel, and live on your terms.

1. THE PRINCIPLES OF Financial Independence

Increase Income Streams: Multiple sources of revenue provide stability.

Live Below Your Means: Spending wisely accelerates wealth-building.

Invest for Growth: Smart investments generate passive income.

Minimize Debt: High-interest debt can slow down financial freedom.

2. STEPS TO ACHIEVE Financial Independence

Step 1: Set Clear Financial Goals

Define how much wealth you need to retire or sustain your lifestyle.

Use the 4% Rule: Estimate annual expenses and invest 25x that amount.

STEP 2: BUILD PASSIVE Income Sources

Invest in stocks, bonds, and REITs for dividends.

Own rental properties to generate cash flow.

Monetize skills through digital products, courses, or freelancing.

STEP 3: MAINTAIN A High Savings Rate

Save at least 30-50% of your income to accelerate growth.

Avoid lifestyle inflation and unnecessary expenses.

STEP 4: DIVERSIFY INVESTMENTS

Spread investments across different asset classes.

Explore alternative income sources like side businesses and royalties.

3. OVERCOMING CHALLENGES on the Path to Wealth

Market Crashes: Have an emergency fund and diversified portfolio.

Unexpected Expenses: Health issues or economic downturns can disrupt plans.

Mindset Shifts: Patience and discipline are key to long-term success.

FINAL ADVICE FOR ACHIEVING Financial Freedom

Start early, but it's never too late to begin.

Focus on long-term growth, not quick riches.

Keep learning about finance and adapting your strategy.

Enjoy the journey—financial independence is about living life on your own terms!

Chapter 41: Living a Rich Life

What Does It Mean to Live a Rich Life?

A truly rich life goes beyond financial wealth. It encompasses financial security, personal fulfillment, strong relationships, and the ability to enjoy and share your success. Living richly means making the most of your resources to create happiness, purpose, and impact.

1. ACHIEVING FINANCIAL Freedom

Ensure that your income covers all needs and allows for future growth.

Build passive income streams to enjoy financial security without constant work.

Maintain smart money habits to sustain long-term wealth.

2. LIVING WITH PURPOSE and Passion

Identify what truly brings you joy and fulfillment.

Invest time in hobbies, travel, and experiences that enrich your life.

Align your financial success with personal goals and meaningful endeavors.

3. BUILDING STRONG Relationships

Prioritize family and friendships over material possessions.

Use your wealth to create unforgettable moments with loved ones.

Practice generosity and support causes that matter to you.

4. GIVING BACK AND Creating Impact

Wealth is most rewarding when shared; consider philanthropy and community contributions.

Support aspiring entrepreneurs, charities, and educational initiatives.

Leave a legacy that benefits future generations.

FINAL WORDS: THE BALANCE of Wealth and Life

A rich life is about balance—financial stability, personal growth, and positive relationships. Continue to seek knowledge, embrace opportunities, and use your wealth to enhance your life and the lives of others.

Your journey to financial success is not just about money, but about living fully and making a difference.

Don't miss out!

Visit the website below and you can sign up to receive emails whenever Arvie Del mundo publishes a new book. There's no charge and no obligation.

https://books2read.com/r/B-A-DNYID-TQDAG

BOOKS 2 READ

Connecting independent readers to independent writers.

About the Publisher

www.ingramcontent.com/pod-product-compliance
Lightning Source LLC
LaVergne TN
LVHW052008160826
845678LV00005B/1681

* 9 7 9 8 2 3 0 8 4 1 6 8 5 *